EXPLORING SCIENCE

CAMERAS

HOW THEY WORK • FILM • DIGITAL • FILTERS • EFFECTS

**With 12 easy-to-do experiments
and 280 exciting pictures**

CHRIS OXLADE

ARMADILLO

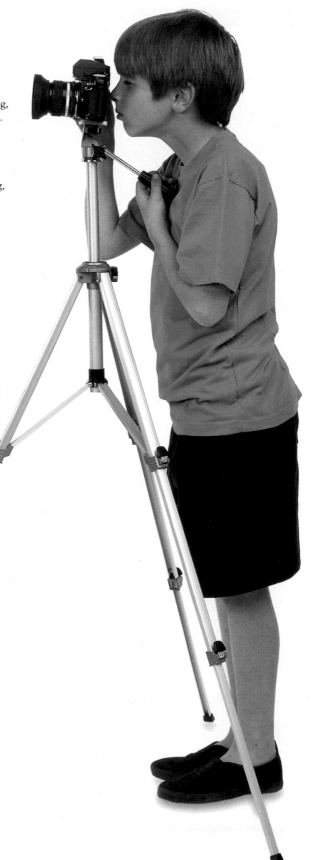

This edition is published by Armadillo, an imprint of Anness Publishing Ltd

info@anness.com; www.armadillobooks.co.uk;
www.annesspublishing.com; twitter: @Anness_Books

If you like the images in this book and would like to investigate using them for publishing,
promotions or advertising, please visit www.practicalpictures.com for more information.

Publisher: Joanna Lorenz
Editors: Joanne Hanks and Joanne Rippin
Consultants: Peter Mellett and John Freeman
Special Photography: John Freeman
Stylist: Marion Elliot
Illustrators: Jerry Fowler, Richard Hawke, John Hutchinson,
Caroline Reeves and Clive Spong
Designers: Caroline Reeves and Ann Samuel
Production Controller: Pirong Wang

PICTURE ACKNOWLEDGEMENTS
(b=bottom, top, m=middle, l=left, r=right)
Aardman Animations Ltd: 56br. Canon UK © Canon: 6mr and br IXUS 155, 7bl EOS
1200D, 11tr EOS 650D, 20tl shutter unit and CMOS sensor EOS 5D, 37ml and 38tr
PowerShot SX40 HS. Corbis: 23tr. Mary Evans: 4bl, 54ml. Flickr: 31bm. Galaxy Picture
Library/Tim Grabham: 61tr. Holt Studios International: 39tl, /Nigel Cattlin: 57br,
60br. iStock: 5tl, tr, bl, 12m, 20mr, 21 all, 30 all, 31tl, tr, ml, 32 all, 33tr, 36bl, 39bl,
50bl, 51t, 55 all, 57mr, 61ml. Robin Kerrod: 61tl. Loreo: 51br. Microscopix: 60r.
Oxford Scientific Films/Scott Camazine: 61bl/Laurence Gould: 50mr. Chris
Oxlade: 49tr. Pinterest: 31bl. The Projection Box: 56tl, 58tr. Science & Society:
9m, 35tr, 56bl, 59br. Science Photo Library: 60bl, /Phillipe Plailly: 51bl,
/Francoise Sauze: 61mr, /Sinclair Stammers: 60tl. Lucy Tizard: 44tl.
Yogile: 31br. Zefa/Powerstock: 5br.

We would like to thank the following pupils from Hampden Gurney
School: Diane, Gary, Kim, Kisanet, Lee, Louisa, Paul, Robert, Sarah
Ann, Shadae, Sheree. Thanks also to Keith Johnson and Pelling Ltd
for the loan of props.

Manufacturer: Anness Publishing Ltd, 108 Great
Russell Street, London WC1B 3NA, England
For Product Tracking go to:
www.annesspublishing.com/tracking
Batch: 7401-23618-1127

CONTENTS

4 • You and your camera

6 • What is a camera?

8 • How a lens works

10 • Experiment with light

12 • Coming into focus

14 • Make your own camera

16 • Film

18 • Recording an image

20 • Image storage

22 • The camera shutter

24 • What an aperture does

26 • The right exposure

28 • Letting in the light

30 • Viewing and sharing images

32 • Printing

34 • Printing and projecting

36 • Wide and narrow

38 • Zooming in and out

40 • Focal lengths

42 • Lighting and flash

44 • Working with light

46 • Filters and effects

48 • Useful tips

50 • Special photography

52 • Amazing effects

54 • Moving pictures

56 • Animation

58 • Easy animation

60 • Cameras in science

62 • Glossary

64 • Index

YOU AND YOUR CAMERA

What is the one essential piece of equipment you shouldn't forget if you are off on a holiday trip or having a birthday party? A camera! It might be a dedicated camera, or it might be the camera on a smartphone or a tablet computer. Cameras are really sophisticated machines that make use of the latest breakthroughs in electronics and optical technology. A camera is designed to do a specific job. It makes a copy of a scene by collecting light from that scene and turning it into a picture. A camera works in a very similar way to your eyes, but it makes a permanent record of the scene instead of simply looking at it.

As simple as blinking
Using a camera is like looking through a special window. Blink your eyes. This is how a camera records light from a scene. A shutter opens to let light pass through a glass lens and fall on to the sensor or film.

With your camera, you can record all kinds of events, such as parties and visits. A simple point-and-shoot compact camera is all you need.

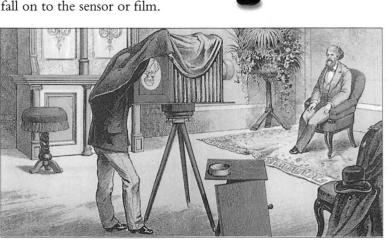

Early cameras
The first practical cameras with film were developed in the 1830s. Today, cameras do the same job, but are much easier to use. In the early days, it could take half an hour to take a photo. Modern cameras have a far shorter exposure time. Scenes can be recorded in a fraction of a second.

Viewing photographs

A camera records images that you can view later. The images taken with a digital camera can be transferred to a computer (such as a tablet computer, *below*), or put on the internet, or printed out on paper (*right*).

The winning picture

If professional photographers are shooting a sports or news event, they must get a clear image. Their pictures appear in magazines and newspapers and help us to understand the story.

Professionals at work

These professional photographers are using telephoto lenses to get a closer picture of the event they are recording. Professionals need to use sophisticated equipment and usually carry two or three cameras, a selection of lenses, a tripod and a flash.

WHAT IS A CAMERA?

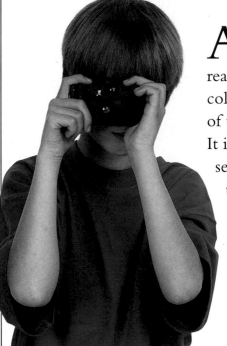

All cameras, from professional film or digital models to simple smartphone cameras, have the same basic parts. The camera body is really just a light-proof box. At the front of the body is the lens, which collects light from the scene and focuses it to make an image in the back of the camera. You see the image on the screen or through a viewfinder. It is recorded by an electronic sensor (or in some cameras by light-sensitive film). Between the lens and the sensor is a shutter. When you take a photograph the shutter opens to let light come through the lens on to the sensor. Many cameras have additional features that help you to take better photographs. For example, the shutter timing and lens position are automatically adjusted to suit different conditions.

Disposable cameras come with the film already inside. You take the whole camera to the film processor when the film is finished.

Inside a film camera

You open the back of a film camera to load and unload the film. There is space for the film cassette and a spool where the used film is stored. The space in the middle is where the image is formed by the lens when the shutter is opened.

shutter release button

flash unit, to light up dark scenes

LCD screen to view digital images or movies

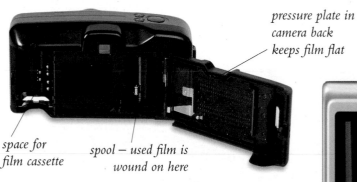

pressure plate in camera back keeps film flat

space for film cassette

spool — used film is wound on here

Compact camera

A compact digital camera is small enough to fit in your pocket. With many models, all you have to do is aim at the scene and press the shutter release button. Simple compacts are also called point-and-shoot cameras. An LCD (liquid-crystal display) screen on the back shows what the camera sees.

Viewing your image

Some compact cameras have a viewfinder that you look through. The view is not quite the same as the view that the lens sees. This is because the viewfinder is higher up than the lens. Remember to leave some space around close-up objects in the viewfinder.

lens view

viewfinder view

You look at a camera's LCD screen, or through the viewfinder, to see what will be in your photo. The guidelines you see in many viewfinders (seen in red here) show you what area of the scene will be included in your picture. If the photographer takes this picture, the boy's hat will be cut off.

Instant photos

The Polaroid camera uses special film which produces prints almost instantly.

DSLR camera

DSLR cameras

Digital single-lens reflex cameras are usually called DSLRs for short. When you look into the viewfinder of a DSLR camera, you see through the lens, so you see what the lens sees. You can change the lens of a DSLR camera to achieve different effects.

HOW A LENS WORKS

Making your own simple viewer will show you just how a camera lens collects light from a scene and makes a small copy of it on the camera's sensor. The copy is called an image. Just like a real camera, the viewer has a light-proof box. At the front of the box is a pin-hole, which works like a tiny lens. The screen at the back of the box is where the sensor would be. This sort of viewer is sometimes called a camera obscura (which just means a dark box used to capture images of outside objects). In the past, artists used these to make images of scenes that they could paint.

MAKE YOUR OWN VIEWER

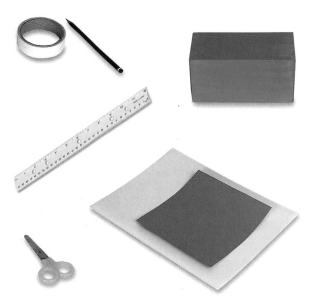

You will need: *ruler, scissors, small cardboard box, card (card stock), sharp pencil, adhesive tape, tracing paper.*

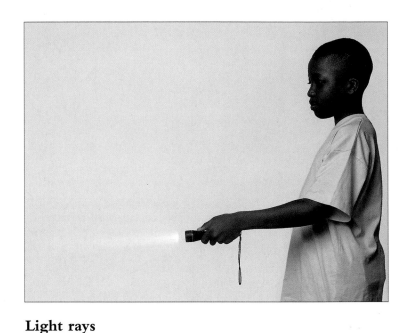

Light rays
Light travels in straight rays. You can see this when you shine a torch (flashlight). When you look at a scene, your eyes collect rays that are coming from every part of it. This is just what a camera does.

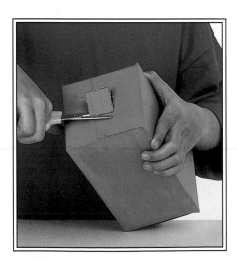

1 Using scissors, cut a small hole, about 1.5x1.5cm/½x½in, in one end of the cardboard box.

2 Now cut a much larger square hole in the other end of your cardboard box.

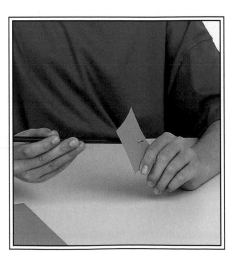

3 Cut a square of card 4x4cm/ 1½x1½in. Pierce a tiny hole in the middle with a sharp pencil.

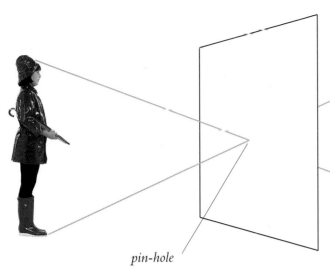

pin-hole

tracing paper screen

If you look at a person through your viewer, light rays from her head hit the bottom of the viewer's screen. Rays from her feet hit the top of the screen. So the screen image is upside down. Left and right are swapped, too.

Making an image with light

When you use your viewer, the pin-hole lets in just a few light rays from each part of the scene. The rays keep going in straight lines and hit the tracing paper screen, making an image of the scene.

A camera obscura

Some camera obscuras are more like rooms than boxes, but they work in the same way. Light from a small hole or simple lens creates a reversed and upside down image on a flat surface. This can be seen in the darkened interior of the room.

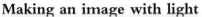

6 Now look out of a window, through the screen of tracing paper. Try tracing the image you see on to the paper.

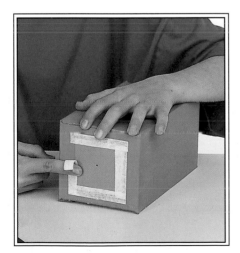

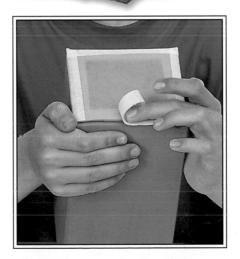

4 Place the card over the box's smaller hole. Make sure that the pin-hole is positioned over the hole. Now tape it into place.

5 Cut a square of tracing paper slightly bigger than the larger hole. Stick it securely over that hole. Your viewer is ready to use.

EXPERIMENT WITH LIGHT

HAVING FUN WITH BEAMS

You will need: ruler, two pieces of card (card stock), scissors, torch (flashlight), glass of water, magnifying glass, mirror.

Light is refracted and reflected inside cameras by lenses and mirrors. The best way to see how this happens is to send some light beams through lenses and then bounce them off mirrors yourself. You can make narrow light beams by shining a torch or flashlight through slots in a sheet of card. Try these experiments and then see if you have any ideas of your own. Vary the size of the slots to see how the light beams change. Carry out the experiments in a darkened room.

Converging light rays

The lens of a magnifying glass makes light rays from objects converge, or bend inwards, towards each other. So, when the rays enter the eye, they seem to have come from a bigger object.

1 Cut a slot about 2mm/⅛in wide and 5cm/2in long in two pieces of card. Bend the bottom edges so they stand up. Shine the light beam of a torch through both.

2 To see how the beam can be refracted put a glass of water in its path. Move the glass from side to side to see how the beam widens and narrows.

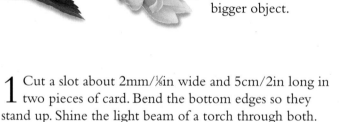

3 Replace the second piece of card with one with three slots in it. Put a magnifying glass in the path of the three beams to make them converge, or bend inwards.

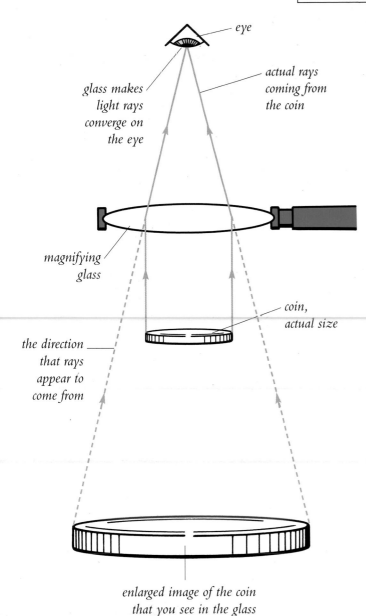

eye

glass makes light rays converge on the eye

actual rays coming from the coin

magnifying glass

the direction that rays appear to come from

coin, actual size

enlarged image of the coin that you see in the glass

Water mirror

Unlike other cameras, single-lens reflex cameras (SLRs) give crisp, clean images. To see why, try this simple experiment. Hold a glass of water up so that you can see the underneath surface of the water clearly. Now poke your finger into the water from above. You should see a clear, single reflection of your finger in the surface. This is because the surface acts just like a mirror (*see box below*).

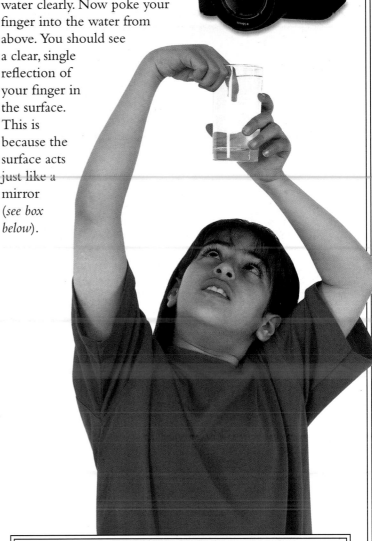

4 Now try each of the experiments, but put a mirror in the way of the different beams. Can you see how the pattern of rays stays the same?

MIRRORS AND PRISMS

Stopping reflections

If you look carefully at a reflection in a normal mirror, you will see a 'ghostly' second image. The water mirror above does not make a 'ghost' image. To stop you from getting 'ghost' images on your pictures, the SLR has a glass block called a pentaprism (a five-angled prism), which treats reflections in the same way as the water mirror.

The same view

The pentaprism in an SLR camera also makes sure that the image you see in the viewfinder is exactly the same as the image on your photo.

COMING INTO FOCUS

Before taking a photograph, you need to make sure that your subject is in focus. When it is, all the rays of light that leave a point on the subject are bent by the lens so that they hit the same place on the sensor or film. This makes a clear, sharp image. Parts of the scene in front of or behind the subject will not be in focus. Most cameras have an autofocus system. When you press the shutter button to take a photograph, the camera adjusts the lens to focus on the part of scene in the middle of the image. Some cameras can even automatically focus on people's faces.

In this photograph (above), the subject is in sharp focus. You can see all the fine detail. When the same shot is out of focus (below), it makes the subject look blurred.

Touchscreen focusing
On cameras and smartphones with a touch-sensitive viewfinder screen, you can choose which part of a scene you want to focus on simply by touching that part of the scene. The camera automatically focuses and takes the photograph.

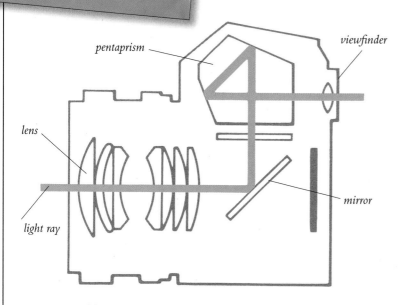

pentaprism

viewfinder

lens

mirror

light ray

Getting closer
Use a magnifying glass and lamp to make an image of an object on a sheet of paper. Move the magnifying glass closer to and farther from the paper, to bring different parts of the scene into focus.

Focusing DSLRs
With a DSLR camera, you see exactly what the image looks like through the viewfinder. This allows you to make sure that the subject of your photograph is perfectly in focus.

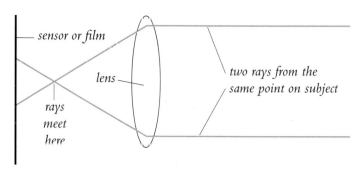

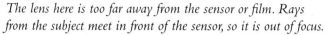

The lens here is too far away from the sensor or film. Rays from the subject meet in front of the sensor, so it is out of focus.

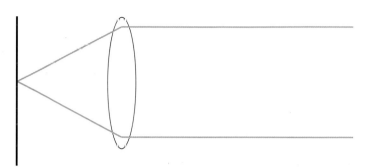

To focus, the lens is moved backwards, towards the sensor or film. The rays now meet on the sensor.

In and out of focus

A camera focuses on a subject by moving the lens backwards and forwards so it gets closer to, or farther from the sensor or film. This brings parts of the scene that are at different distances from the camera into focus. When the lens is set closest to the sensor, objects from the distance are in sharper focus.

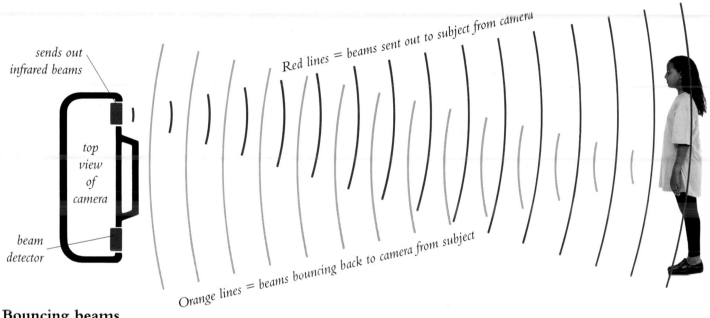

sends out
infrared beams

top
view
of
camera

beam
detector

Red lines = beams sent out to subject from camera

Orange lines = beams bouncing back to camera from subject

Bouncing beams

With the type of autofocus system shown here, the camera emits a wide beam of invisible infrared light. It works out how long the infrared light takes to bounce back, and so knows how far away the subject is. A small electric motor then moves the lens.

Autofocus errors

Most autofocus cameras focus on objects that are in the middle of the scene in the viewfinder. If your subject is off to one side, the camera focuses on the background, and your subject will be blurred (*left*). If you have a focus lock, you can beat this by aiming at the subject first, and then using your focus lock before recomposing the shot and shooting (*right*).

MAKE YOUR OWN CAMERA

MAKE A PIN-HOLE CAMERA

You will need: *pin-hole box viewer, kitchen foil, scissors, adhesive tape, pencil, black paper, thin card (card stock), thick cloth or plastic, photographic paper, rubber band.*

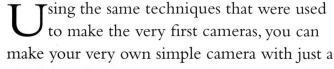

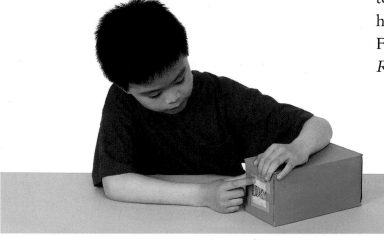

Using the same techniques that were used to make the very first cameras, you can make your very own simple camera with just a few basic pieces of equipment. This project combines all the main principles that lie behind photography. For simplicity, this camera uses photographic paper (paper with a light-sensitive coating on one side) instead of film, and a pin-hole instead of a lens. When the 'film' (paper) is processed, you will have a negative. Then turn to the *Printing and Projecting* project to find out how you can make a print from the negative. Find out about the equipment you need in the *Recording an Image* project.

1 Make the pin-hole viewer from the *How a Lens Works* project, but remove the tracing-paper screen. Replace the 4cm/1½in card square with kitchen foil. Pierce a hole, 2mm/⅛in across, in the middle of the foil with a sharp pencil.

2 Open the back of the box and line the inside with black paper. Alternatively, darken the inside with a black felt pen.

3 Cut a square of card large enough to cover the kitchen foil. Tape just the top edge to the box, so that it will act as a shutter.

4 Cut a square of card to fit right across the other end of the box. Tape it to one edge so that it closes over the hole like a door or flap.

5 Find some heavy, black, light-proof cloth or a plastic sheet. Cut a piece large enough to fold around the end of the box.

6 In a completely dark room, feeling with your fingers, put a piece of photographic paper under the flap at the end of the box.

7 Close the flap, then wrap the cloth or plastic sheet tightly over it. Next, put a rubber band tightly around the box to secure it.

8 Now you can turn the light on. Point the camera at a well-lit object and open the shutter. Leave the camera still for about 5 minutes and then close the shutter.

Throwaway camera
Single-use cameras have the film already loaded and ready to use. You send off the whole camera when you want the film to be developed.

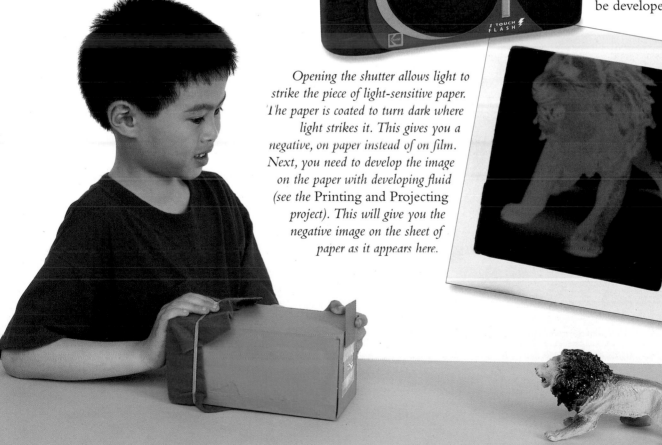

Opening the shutter allows light to strike the piece of light-sensitive paper. The paper is coated to turn dark where light strikes it. This gives you a negative, on paper instead of on film. Next, you need to develop the image on the paper with developing fluid (see the Printing and Projecting *project). This will give you the negative image on the sheet of paper as it appears here.*

FILM

In the early 1990s nearly all cameras still used film to record images. Digital cameras were very expensive. Ten years later most cameras sold were digital cameras. Today, film is used mainly by some enthusiasts and professional photographers, and in throw-away cameras. However, you can still buy film to put in film cameras. Photographic film is made up of thin transparent plastic sheet coated with light-sensitive chemicals. The film must be kept in the dark until it is exposed in the camera. When you take a photograph with a film camera, the image falls on the film. The light makes the chemicals change, and so the image is recorded.

Types of film

The three main types of film are colour print film, black and white film, and slide film. Both print film and black and white film produce a negative image, which is then used to make prints. Slide film produces a transparent photograph that is used for projecting.

Film is stored in light-tight canisters.

A developed strip of colour negative film

Film formats

Different film cameras take photographs in different shapes and sizes, called formats. The most common format is 35mm, so called because the film strip is 35mm (about 1⅜in) wide. A standard roll of 35mm film has room for 24 or 36 photographs, or frames. Films also come in different speeds, called ISO ratings. Most films are medium speed, rated at 100 or 200 ISO.

disk camera film

35mm film

APS film

110 film

126 cartridge

120 film

The film is exposed by the camera when you photograph something, such as this bird, against a light background.

lens   film

Exposing film

When a film is exposed in a camera, the chemicals in the film respond very rapidly, so a photograph can be taken in a fraction of a second. The brighter the light that shines on the film, the more the chemicals change. So the chemicals change more in the lighter areas of the image than the darker areas. The film must be kept in the dark to prevent the image from being spoiled, so when the film is used up, it is wound back into its light-proof canister before being removed from the camera.

latent image

crystals in this sky area are exposed to light

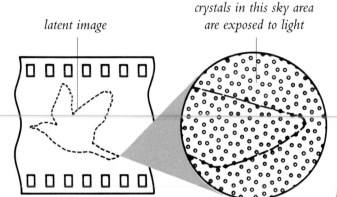

Crystals in the light area of the image change. Crystals in the dark area do not. The image has been recorded chemically. It is called the latent (hidden) image. Nothing shows up on the film until it is processed.

Polaroid film

The film used in Polaroid cameras is very different from other films. As well as the chemicals to record the image, it has developing chemicals inside. After a photograph is taken, the film is squeezed through a roller, which releases the developer. This turns the film into a finished photograph.

Processing film

Film must be processed after exposure. Processing is done in several stages. First the film is developed using chemicals, to make the image appear on the film. The next stage is fixing, which gets rid of left-over chemicals, so the image can't change. Then the film is washed and dried.

Film can be developed at home in a small developing tank.

FACT BOX

• Infrared film is coated with chemicals that react to heat, rather than to the visible light rays, coming from a scene.

• The largest print photograph in the world measures 9.58m/31ft high by 32.74m/107ft wide. To take it, an abandoned aircraft hangar in Irvine, California, USA, was used as the world's largest pin-hole camera.

• 35mm format film was originally developed for movie cameras. It is still the most common format for movie camera film.

RECORDING AN IMAGE

MAKE A PHOTOGRAM

You will need: *lamp, photographic paper, different-shaped objects such as keys, discs and scissors, rubber gloves, protective goggles, plastic tongs, plastic dishes, chemicals (see below).*

Photographic chemicals

You will need two photographic chemicals: developer for paper (not film) and fixer. Buy them from a photographic supplier. Ask an adult to help you follow the instructions on the bottles to dilute (mix with water) the chemicals and make sure you protect your eyes and hands when handling them. Store the diluted chemicals in plastic bottles. Seal the bottles and label them clearly.

You do not need a camera to see how film works. In fact, you do not need a film either. You can use black and white photographic paper instead.

Photographic paper is the paper that prints are made on. It works in the same way as film. Here, you can see how to make a picture called a photogram. It is made by covering some parts of a sheet of photographic paper with objects and then shining light on the sheet. When the paper is developed, the areas that were hit by the light turn black, leaving you an image of the objects.

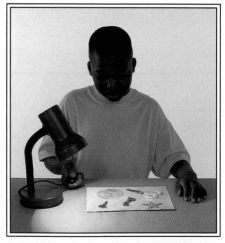

1 Turn off the light. Lay a sheet of photographic paper down, shiny side up. Put objects on it. Turn the light on again for a few seconds.

2 Pick up the paper with the tongs and put it into the dish of developer. Push it down so that the paper is all under the liquid.

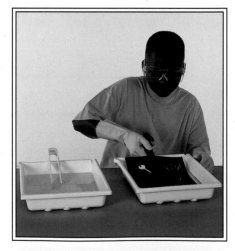

3 After a minute, use the tongs to move the paper into the fixer. Leave it right under the liquid for a minute, until the image is fixed.

This symbol, on photographic chemical bottles, means that they can be dangerous if not used with care. Always wear gloves and goggles.

Photographic paper

For black and white prints, you need a paper called monochrome paper. Buy the smallest size you can, and choose grade 2 if possible, with a gloss finish. The paper comes in a light-proof envelope or box. Open the envelope only in complete darkness. The paper is in a second, black plastic envelope.

The finished photogram should show the objects in white on a black background. Try experimenting with other ideas. How about cutting out letters and making your name, or crumpling up transparent materials to create more exciting effects?

4 Now you can turn the light back on. Using the tongs, lift the paper out of the fixer and wash it with running water for a few minutes. Then lay the paper on a flat surface to dry. This technique is an excellent way of producing unique invitations or greetings cards quickly and effectively.

IMAGE STORAGE

Shutter unit

CMOS sensor

Y̵ou've seen how the lens of a camera focuses light from a scene to make a small image of the scene. Now the camera needs to record the image to turn it into a photograph that you can keep. Nearly all modern cameras record images digitally. The image falls on to a special light-sensitive microchip called an image sensor. The sensor divides the image into millions of tiny dots called pixels, and measures the colour and brightness of each one. These measurements are turned into numbers and then put together to make a digital image file, which is stored on a memory chip.

A CCD image sensor

Image sensors

A sensor is a very complex electronic circuit built into a silicon chip, and mounted in a plastic case. Sensors are either CCD (charge-coupled device) or CMOS (complementary metal-oxide semiconductor) sensors. Sensors come in different sizes, but in a DSLR the top surface of a sensor chip is about 2cm/1in across. It has a grid of millions of microscopic, light-recording devices called photosites. Each photosite represents one pixel of the captured image. In a camera, light is focused on to this surface when you take a photograph. The brightness of the light changes the amount of electricity in each component. So the sensor records the brightness of different parts of the image. To generate a colour image, a thin filter is placed over the layer of photosites. The filter is a mosaic of red, green and blue squares, with each square sitting directly above a photodiode. With this in place, each photosite is able to record varying intensities of red, green or blue light.

Millions of photodiodes cover a digital sensor. A coloured filter enables it to record colour, while the microlens optimizes the light from the camera lens.

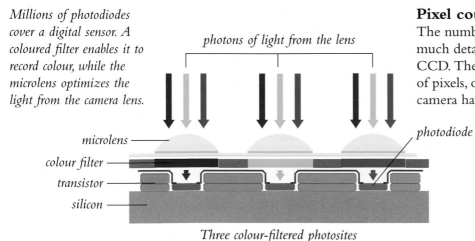

photons of light from the lens

microlens
colour filter
transistor
silicon
photodiode

Three colour-filtered photosites

Pixel counts

The number of pixels on a CCD determines how much detail will be in an image recorded by the CCD. The number of pixels is measured in millions of pixels, or megapixels. A typical high-end digital camera has a CCD with around 24 megapixels, which means the camera's sensor has approximately 24 million photosites. Each image has 6000 pixels horizontally and 4000 pixels vertically. To work out the number of megapixels in an image, multiply the number of pixels horizontally by the number of pixels vertically.

From sensor to memory

As soon as the camera shutter closes, the camera takes the information from the sensor and processes it to create an image file. The amount of electricity in each pixel is measured and turned into a number that represents the colour and brightness of the light that hit that pixel. The image file is transferred to memory. This all happens in a fraction of a second.

Images can be taken with in-camera special effects such as soft focus (left), sepia (above), and black-and-white tones. The sepia tones resemble the effect of aging in old photographs. Most digital cameras include a sepia tone option.

Memory cards

In a digital camera the images are stored on memory cards, mostly in a format called JPEG. The cards can hold hundreds or thousands of JPEG images. The more pixels in each image, the more memory the image takes up on a card. Once full, a card can be swapped for an empty card.

Secure Digital (SD) memory cards

CompactFlash memory cards

All shapes and sizes

Digital memory cards or flash cards come in all shapes and sizes, but they serve the same purpose, which is to store images. The main types of memory card are Secure Digital (SD) – these are small in size and are easily available with memory capacity ranging from 4GB to 64GB. Micro and mini SD cards are designed for smaller devices, and CompactFlash (CF) is a larger and stronger card that can hold up to 256GB.

THE CAMERA SHUTTER

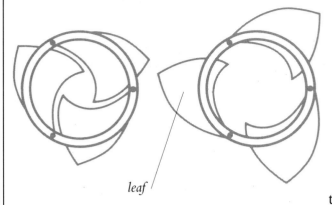

leaf

A leaf shutter has thin metal plates called leaves. These overlap each other to close the shutter (left) and swivel back to open it (right).

Many cameras have a shutter between the lens at the front and the sensor or film at the back. The shutter is rather like a door. It is closed most of the time, so that no light gets to the sensor. When you press the button to take a photo, the shutter opens briefly to let light from your subject reach the sensor. Some shutters, called leaf shutters, are part of the lens, while others, called focal-plane shutters, are at the back of the camera. Compact digital cameras and smartphones don't have shutters. The sensor is simply turned on and off to take a photograph. The time for which the shutter is open is called the shutter speed.

first curtain

Focal-plane shutter

This has two curtains. When the camera takes a photograph, the first curtain opens to let light hit the sensor or film. The second curtain follows closely behind, covering up the sensor again. The smaller the gap between the curtains, the faster the shutter speed.

second curtain

Shutter speeds

The speed with which a shutter moves is measured in fractions of a second. Most photographs are taken with shutter speeds between 1/60 and 1/500 of a second. Most cameras will decide the best shutter speed for you automatically, depending on the subject you are photographing, but you can also choose the shutter speed you want. The opening of the shutter determines the amount of time light is allowed to pass through the lens to the sensor.

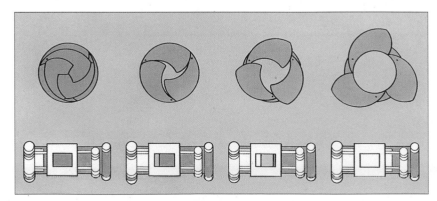

A leaf shutter (top) and a focal plane shutter (bottom) are shown, step by step, in the process of opening.

Camera shake

When the shutter is open, even tiny camera movements make the image move across the film, causing a slightly blurred picture. This is called camera shake. Many cameras have an image stabilization system to reduce shake.

A tripod forms a steady base for a camera. It is very useful if you are taking photographs with slow shutter speeds because there is no chance of camera shake. Using a tripod will also help you to compose your pictures really well, because you do not have to worry about holding the camera. You can also vary the height of your viewpoint.

This image shows the track and field sprinter Christine Arron in action. The photographer has panned the camera (moved it to follow the athlete), which blurs the background, enhancing the impression of speed.

Panning, or moving, your camera to follow a moving subject helps to stop the subject from being blurred. The stationary elements (background) of the photo will still appear fuzzy.

When you photograph action, such as people running, a fast shutter speed will freeze the action, and avoid a blurred shot. Panning will also help, especially if your subject is moving across the scene. To pan, aim at your subject and swing the camera to follow it, squeezing the shutter release button when the subject is where you want it.

There are several ways of keeping your camera steady as you take a photograph, even if you do not have a tripod. For example, stand with your legs slightly apart, or crouch down with one knee on the ground. Squeeze the shutter release button slowly. For extra steadiness, lean yourself against a tree, or try resting your camera on a wall. A friend's shoulder or bean bag are also good ideas.

WHAT AN APERTURE DOES

The aperture ring on an SLR lens. Aperture size is measured in f-numbers (such as f/8).

The aperture is basically a hole, situated behind the camera lens, that can be made larger or smaller. When the aperture is small, some of the light rays that pass through the lens are cut off so that they do not reach the sensor or film. This reduces the amount of light that reaches the sensor. Changing the size of the aperture also affects how much of the scene is in focus, which is important for taking shots such as portraits. Most smartphones have cameras with a fixed aperture.

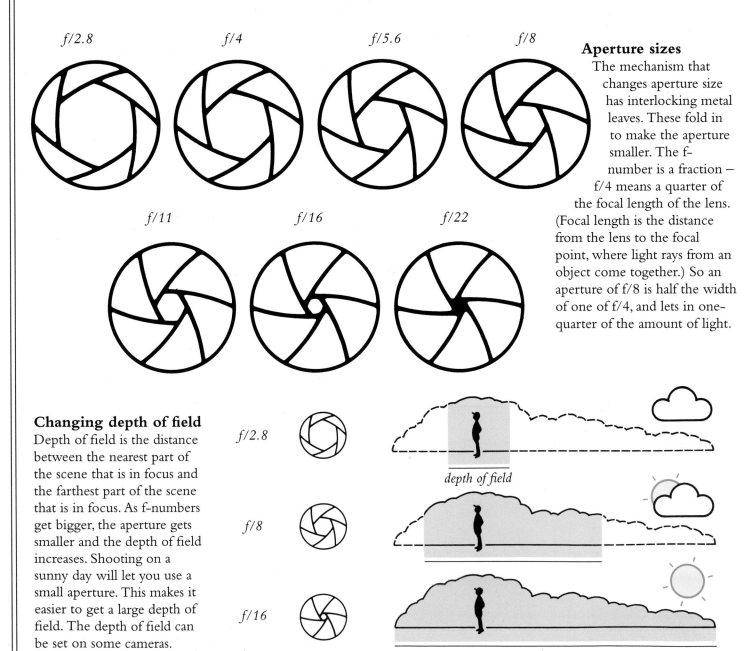

f/2.8   f/4   f/5.6   f/8

f/11   f/16   f/22

Aperture sizes
The mechanism that changes aperture size has interlocking metal leaves. These fold in to make the aperture smaller. The f-number is a fraction – f/4 means a quarter of the focal length of the lens. (Focal length is the distance from the lens to the focal point, where light rays from an object come together.) So an aperture of f/8 is half the width of one of f/4, and lets in one-quarter of the amount of light.

Changing depth of field
Depth of field is the distance between the nearest part of the scene that is in focus and the farthest part of the scene that is in focus. As f-numbers get bigger, the aperture gets smaller and the depth of field increases. Shooting on a sunny day will let you use a small aperture. This makes it easier to get a large depth of field. The depth of field can be set on some cameras.

f/2.8

f/8

f/16

depth of field

This photograph was taken with a much smaller aperture than the photograph on the far left, making the depth of field far deeper. Almost everything in the scene is in focus. Greater depth of field is useful for photographs of scenery or architecture where you want to show clear detail. It is also useful if you have people in the foreground and want both the people and the background to be in focus.

In this photograph, the subject (the children) is in focus, and the background is totally out of focus. This is called a shallow depth of field because only the objects that are a certain distance from the camera are in focus. Using shallow depth of field is ideal if you want to make parts of the scene that might confuse your picture disappear into a blur.

FACT BOX

• A lens always has its maximum aperture written on it. For example, a lens described as 300 f/4 has a focal length of 300mm and a maximum aperture of f/4.

• Large maximum apertures tend to be very expensive, because the lenses have to be much bigger. For example, an f/1.4 lens can cost several times as much as an f/4 lens.

• A pin-hole camera the size of a shoe-box has an aperture of about f/500 (1/500th of the focal length).

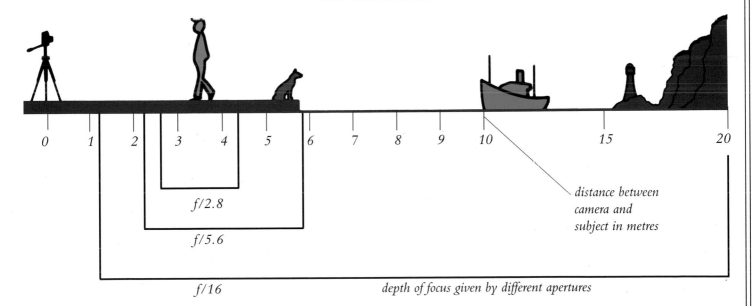

| 0 | 1 | 2 | 3 | 4 | 5 | 6 | 7 | 8 | 9 | 10 | 15 | 20 |

f/2.8

f/5.6

distance between camera and subject in metres

f/16　　　　*depth of focus given by different apertures*

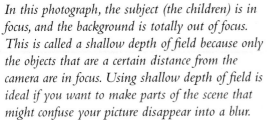

Try focusing your camera at a certain object and then changing the aperture. You will see how different areas of the picture come into focus.

Lens focused at 3m/9ft
Aperture at f/2.8
Depth of field=1.5m/5ft

Lens focused at 3m/9ft
Aperture at f/5.6
Depth of field=3.5m/11½ft

Lens focused at 3m/9ft
Aperture at f/16
Depth of field=20m/65ft

THE RIGHT EXPOSURE

Exposure is the word for the amount of light that reaches the sensor or film in your camera when you take a photograph. Exposure depends on the shutter speed (slower shutter speeds give more time and allow more light through) and the aperture (larger apertures also allow more light through). You might see exposure stated on your camera as a combination of shutter speed and aperture, for example, f/16 at 1/60 sec. All but the simplest cameras measure the amount of light coming from the scene and work out what exposure is needed for the speed of the film in the camera. They do this with an electronic light sensor called a metering system.

In this picture, too little light has reached the sensor. This is called underexposure. Either the shutter speed was too fast, or the aperture was too small. The photograph looks too dark.

Here, too much light has fallen on the sensor. This is called overexposure. Either the shutter speed was too slow, or the aperture was too large. The light areas of the photograph are washed out.

When this photograph was taken, the exposure was correct and exactly the right amount of light reached the sensor. The finished picture is well-balanced – neither too light, nor too dark.

Shutter speed and aperture

The exposure always needs to be correct to produce a good photograph. The correct exposure can be achieved by different combinations of shutter speed and aperture, each of which lets in the same amount of light (*see right*). You might use the F16 aperture for a landscape to get a good depth of field, but the 1/500 sec shutter speed for an action shot. A camera's scene settings can automatically choose the correct combination for you.

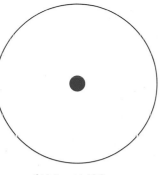

f/16 at 1/30 sec

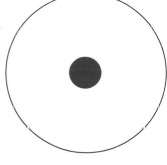

f/8 at 1/125 sec

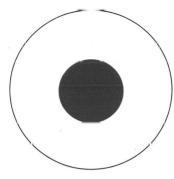

f/4 at 1/500 sec

FACT BOX

- Most cameras have different light metering settings, so they can measure the brightness of different parts of the scene, or the whole scene.

- In digital cameras, the shutter and aperture settings used by the camera are stored in the image file so you can check what they were later.

- It's more important to get the exposure correct in a film camera than a digital camera, because the image can't be adjusted later.

In the picture on the left, the light shining through the window is brighter than the main subject – the girl. This means that the camera measures more of the light coming from the brighter area. As a result, the background is correctly exposed, but the girl is underexposed and so she looks too dark.

In this picture, the background was still by far the brightest part of the picture. The problem was solved, however, by using a much larger exposure and the balance is just right. Bright light coming from the background is called back lighting.

LETTING IN THE LIGHT

Changing a camera's aperture affects both the brightness of an image and the depth of field. You can see how it works with a few simple experiments. First, look at your own eyes. Like an aperture, your pupils automatically narrow in bright light to protect your retinas, and open wide to let you see in dim light. To see a shutter at work, you can open the back of a film camera (when there is no film in it). Now look for a leaf shutter near the lens or a focal-plane shutter just behind where the film would be.

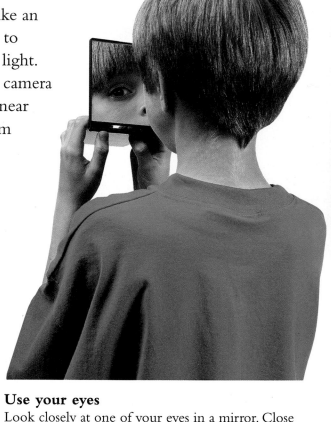

INVESTIGATING APERTURES

You will need: magnifying glass, cardboard tube, adhesive tape, scissors, thin card (card stock), tracing paper, table lamp, pencil.

Use your eyes
Look closely at one of your eyes in a mirror. Close it and, after a few seconds, open it again quickly. You should see your pupil go from wide to narrow as your eye adjusts to the bright light.

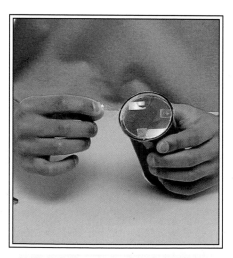

1 Carefully attach the magnifying glass to one end of your cardboard tube using small pieces of adhesive tape.

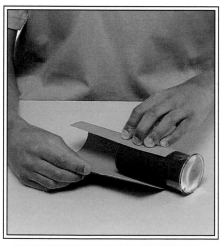

2 Roll a piece of thin card around the other end of the tube. Tape the top edge down to make another tube that slides in and out.

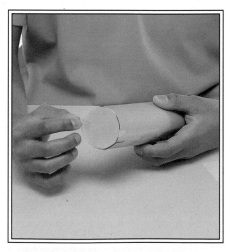

3 With adhesive tape, attach a circle of tracing paper across the end of the sliding card tube. This will form your viewing screen.

See a shutter at work

To see just how a shutter works, open the back of an old film camera (when there is no film inside) and carefully place a small strip of tracing paper where the film would be. Now aim the camera at a subject, preferably one that is brightly lit, and press the shutter release button. You should see a brief flash of the image on your tracing paper – although there will be no lasting picture. Take great care not to put your fingers on the delicate shutter blades in the focal-plane cameras.

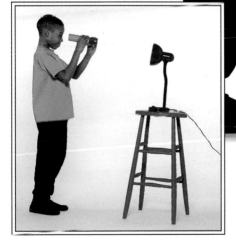

4 With the screen nearest to you, aim your tube at a table lamp that is turned on. Can you see an image of the bulb on the screen?

5 Slide the tubes together until the image of the bulb is clear. Now adjust them again so that the image is slightly out of focus.

6 Mark then cut a small hole (about 5mm/¼in wide) in a piece of card, to make a small aperture. Look at the light bulb again and put the card in front of the lens. The smaller aperture will bring the light bulb into focus. Is it clearer? Can you read the writing on the bulb?

VIEWING AND SHARING IMAGES

The fun part of taking photographs is sharing them so your family and friends can see what you've been up to. The easiest way to share photographs is to show them on a screen. That might be the screen of your camera, smartphone, tablet, computer or television. You can also print photographs on paper to put in albums or stick on the wall (see the next page for more about printing). You can store digital photographs on the internet so that anyone can view them if you give them permission.

Camera to computer

Many people store all their photographs on a personal computer. There are various ways of downloading (copying) the photographs from the camera's memory card to the computer, including along a USB cable, by plugging the memory card into the computer, and wirelessly by Bluetooth or over a network.

Online storage

On the internet are many photo-sharing sites. You can copy, or upload, thousands of photographs from your computer to these sites. Making the photographs public means that people anywhere in the world can look at your snaps. You can also store your photos in 'the cloud'. That means they are stored on the internet, and you can view them on any of your devices. You can also share them with your friends and family so that they can see what you are up to, wherever you are and whatever you're doing.

Taking 'selfies' is now a part of many people's everyday life. Sites like Instagram and Snapchat let you share what you're doing, and who you're with, just seconds after you take the photograph.

Viewing and editing

Personal computers have software for viewing photographs, and showing them as slideshows. You can also connect a projector to a computer, and connect a computer to a television, for seeing the photographs on a large scale. This software also allows simple editing, such as cropping photographs or changing their colour.

Photos on social media

People like to show their photographs on social media, such as Facebook and Twitter. Photos taken from smartphones and some of the latest cameras can be uploaded straight to social-media websites. There are also websites, like Pinterest, Flickr, Yogile and others, that offer storage and album facilities. The albums you create can be shared with other people, who can also add their photographs.

Safety online

When sharing images online, always ask a responsible adult for permission before you begin. Choose a user name that isn't your own and only share your passwords with a parent or carer. Don't post any personal information, like your address or where you go to school. Think carefully about posting an image of yourself or your friends. Remember that once it's online it might be viewed by people you don't know.

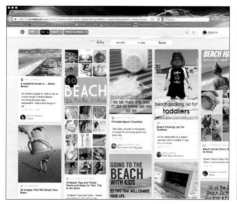

Web pages from (left to right) *Pinterest, Flickr and Yogile*

PRINTING

One way to view photographs is to print them out on paper. This makes a permanent record of the image. Collections of photographs can be collected in albums. Prints are also made for decorating walls and for exhibitions of photographers' work. There are many ways of getting images from a camera on to paper to make a print. You can print digital image files on a colour printer attached to a computer. If you want to make lots of prints, you can take a memory stick to a shop that has a printing machine, or order prints online.

Printing at home

Colour printers print using different coloured inks (normally cyan, magenta, yellow and black), which can be combined to produce almost any colour. Printing on glossy photo paper produces very good results. As well as printing from a personal computer, you can also print directly to a printer from most digital cameras by plugging the camera into the printer, or by inserting the memory card from the camera into the printer.

When you have a collection of special photographs, you might like to create an album.

If your home printer has a wi-fi connection, you can print direct from a mobile device or a tablet.

Online printing

Online printing services allow you to upload your photographs to a website to be printed in high quality and posted to you. This is normally cheaper than printing lots of photos with a home printer. Online printing services also let you print very large photographs on paper and on canvas. They also allow you to put your photographs together to make books and calendars, which you can design yourself using a website. Your photographs can also be put on mugs, T-shirts, table mats and other objects to make fun gifts.

Printing from film

When colour negative film and black and white film is developed, the images are in negative form. They have to be printed so that you can see the photographs. To make a print, light is shone through the film and focused on to light-sensitive paper. This is done in a darkened room. Then the film is developed to make the photograph appear.

Enlarging is the first stage in making a print. An enlarger projects the negative on to paper placed below it. This must be done in the dark, so that no stray light spoils the paper. Lighter areas of the negative allow more light to reach the paper than darker areas.

The paper is processed in the dark, using chemicals. The three trays hold the developer, water or stop bath (to stop the developer) and fixer. Areas where light has hit the paper come out dark. So light areas of the negative come out dark, as in the original scene.

After processing, the final print must be dried carefully, to prevent it from getting scratched or curling at the edges. Once developed, take care of your prints by mounting them on card (card stock) using a glue such as photo spray mount. You can then frame the pictures you like the best, or keep them in a photograph album.

PROJECT

PRINTING AND PROJECTING

QUICK AND EASY PRINTS

You will need: *photographic paper and chemicals, negative from pin-hole camera, torch (flashlight) or table lamp, safety goggles, rubber gloves, plastic dishes, plastic tongs or tweezers.*

If you have taken a photograph with your own pin-hole camera, you can find out how to turn it into a print below. There is also a simple projector for you to make.

A projector allows you to look at photographs on a large scale. There are digital projectors that can be attached to computers, and slide projectors for looking at slide film. Projecting a slide is rather like the reverse of taking a photograph. First, light is shone through the slide. It then passes through the lens of the projector and is focused on a flat surface such as a wall, where an enlarged version appears.

A slide viewer is a special magnifying glass with an opalescent (milky-colour) screen used for looking at slides. It is an alternative to a projector. You can also use a light box (a glass box with a light inside) to look at your slides before viewing in a projector.

1 In a totally dark room, lay a fresh sheet of photographic paper on a flat surface, shiny side up. Lay the negative from your pin-hole camera face-down on top.

2 Shine a torch or a table lamp on to the top of the two papers for a few seconds. Turn the torch off and remove your paper negative. Put on the goggles and gloves.

3 Put the fresh paper into a tray of developing fluid, then fix and wash the fresh paper (see the previous page). You should end up with a print of the original image.

DO-IT-YOURSELF PROJECTOR

You will need: *cardboard tube, scissors, developed colour negative film, thin card (card stock), adhesive tape, magnifying glass, tracing paper, torch (flashlight).*

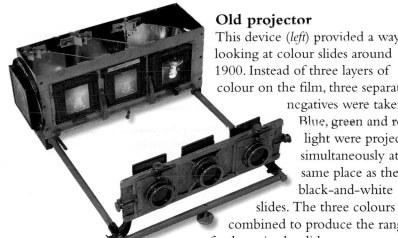

Old projector

This device (*left*) provided a way of looking at colour slides around 1900. Instead of three layers of colour on the film, three separate negatives were taken. Blue, green and red light were projected simultaneously at the same place as the black-and-white slides. The three colours combined to produce the range of colours in the slide scene.

1 Cut two slits either side of the cardboard tube at one end. They must be wide enough for a strip of negatives to slide through. Only use old negatives that you do not want.

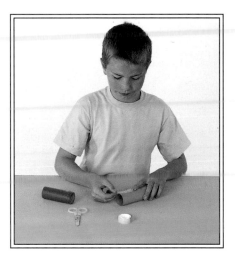

2 Wrap a piece of card around the other end of the tube. Tape down the edge to make another tube that slides over the first tube.

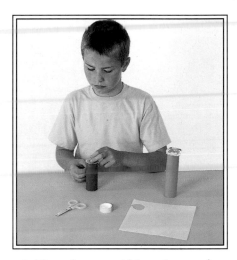

3 Tape the magnifying glass to the end of the adjustable tube. Now tape a disc of tracing paper over the slotted end of the main tube.

4 Hold the projector about 2m/6ft away from a pale wall or screen. Slot the negative into the tube and shine a torch through it. Adjust the tubes until an image of the negative appears on the wall. You can also try this with slide film, but only use old, unwanted slides.

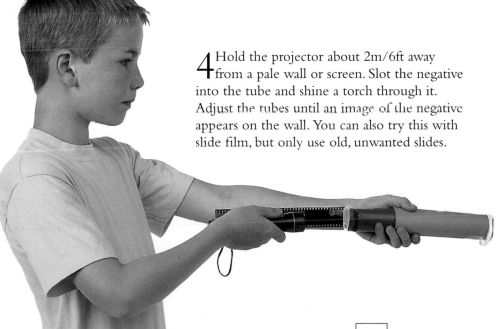

the image as projected on the wall or screen

WIDE AND NARROW

All camera lenses have their own focal length, which is written on the lens. The focal length is the distance between the middle of the lens and the focal plane inside, where the lens creates an image of the object being photographed on the sensor or film. On a digital SLR, if you use a 50mm lens, the image you see is the same scene you see with your eyes. Lenses of different focal lengths produce images that make the objects in the scene closer or further away than they actually are. Lenses with shorter focal lengths take in more of the scene, and longer lenses take in less than you would normally see.

What the lens sees

Put your hands either side of your face. Your view is similar to what a 50mm lens can see. Keeping your hands the same distance apart, move your hands steadily away from your face. The view between your hands will show you what a telephoto lens sees.

A wide angle lens has a wider angle of view (about 50% more) than the human eye.

Only light rays that pass through the very middle remain straight.

Ultra-wide angle

The widest type of lens collects light from a complete half-circle (180 degrees). It makes straight lines appear curved, and the middle of the scene seems to bulge outwards. It is called a fish-eye lens because fish have eyes that gather light from a huge angle.

Long-lens wobble

With telephoto lenses, which have very long focal lengths (300mm or more), the tiniest bit of camera shake blurs the image. Professionals usually use a tripod or monopod with these lenses, to keep the camera steady. This is also important because the amount of light that reaches the lens is quite small, and so slow shutter speeds are often needed.

A normal view

The simplest cameras, including the cameras on smartphones and tablets, usually give a slightly wider view (*left*) than you see with your own eyes. Most digital compact cameras have a zoom lens that allows you to get a closer shot of your subject while you are still far away from it. These are especially useful for taking portraits (see *Zooming In and Out* to find out more).

Compact digital camera with zoom lens.

The view through a telephoto lens.

Telephoto lens view

Any lens that gives you a magnified view of a scene is called a telephoto lens. A telephoto lens is a bit like a telescope, because it homes in on just one part of the scene. Telephoto lenses are often used to photograph portraits and distant wildlife, and for coming in close on the small details in a scene.

A wide-angle lens view.

Wide-angle lenses

Any camera lens that gives a wider view than we usually see with our eyes is called a wide-angle lens. Extremely wide-angle lenses (of 28mm and less) allow you to get a huge amount of a scene into your photograph. A really wide-angle lens is perfect to use for panoramic photographs of scenery – such as cityscapes.

ZOOMING IN AND OUT

A zoom lens has an adjustable focal length, so it can show anything from a wide angle of view to a narrow angle of view. It allows you to change how much of a scene will be in a photograph without having to move your body. The built-in lens on most compact cameras is a zoom lens, and there are zoom lenses for digital SLR cameras. A typical compact camera may have a '20x' zoom. That means the longest focal length of the lens is twenty times its shortest focal length. Sometimes you might want to take a photograph of a very small object, such as a flower or insect. For that, you need a special lens called a macro lens, which allows you to get really close in without getting a blurred photograph. Many cameras have a macro setting that allows you to get close-up shots.

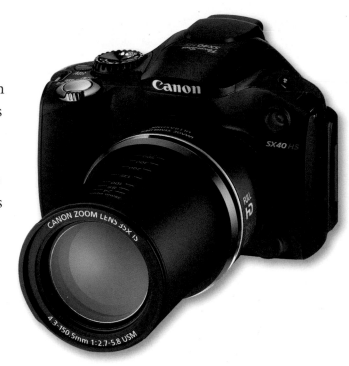

Optical and digital zoom
Most digital cameras have optical zoom and digital zoom. Optical zoom uses the lens to close in on a subject. Digital zoom gives you a longer telephoto shot by cropping the image on the sensor.

A photograph taken at the 28mm setting on a 28–200 zoom lens.

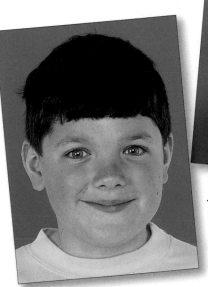

Zoomed in for detail with a 200mm setting.

DSLR zooms
With a DSLR you can use different zoom lenses because the lenses can be swapped over. With two zooms, such as an 18–55 (meaning focal lengths from 18mm to 55mm), and a 55–200, you can go from very wide angle (18mm) to long telephoto (200mm). On these zoom lenses, the focal length is changed by turning or sliding a wide ring on the lens. Because zoom lenses are so complicated, they can make straight lines in a scene look slightly bent, especially at the picture's edges.

Getting really close

A macro setting on a camera or lens allows you to get quite close to objects you want to photograph. But to get really close, you need a camera with interchangeable lenses, and a special attachment called an extension tube, which fits between the camera and the lens. This moves the lens away from the sensor.

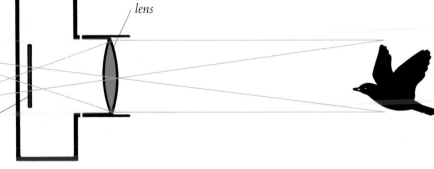

Extension tubes

Extension tubes fit between the camera body and the lens. They move the lens farther from the film. This means that the lens can bend light rays into focus from objects that would usually be too close. A set of extension tubes has three tubes of different lengths for different magnifications.

extension tubes

image falls behind sensor

lens

Usually, the light rays from a close-up object are not bent enough to form a focused image.

sensor

With an extension tube, the lens moves forward, giving room for the rays to become focused.

image focused on sensor

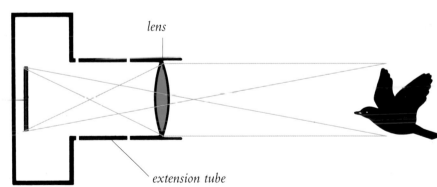

lens

extension tube

Zooming in for a close-up on a face is especially effective when taking portraits of people.

FACT BOX

- A telephoto doubler fits between a DSLR and its lens. It doubles the focal length of the lens.

- A professional 500mm telephoto lens with a maximum aperture of f/8 weighs several kilograms!

- The longest lenses you can buy have a focal length of 1000–1200mm.

- A standard lens might be made up of five glass lenses. Most zoom lenses contain at least twelve lenses.

FOCAL LENGTHS

If you have either an SLR camera or a compact camera with a zoom lens, then you will probably have taken photographs at different focal lengths. The simple experiments shown on these two pages will help to explain how different focal lengths make more or less of a scene appear on the sensor or film. These will help you to give more impact to your pictures. In the mini experiment on the left, try to find as many convex lenses as you can to experiment with. You will find that weaker lenses, which have longer focal lengths, make larger images. This is the opposite to what happens if you use them as a magnifying glass.

Working with lenses
Standing by a window, use a magnifying glass to form an image of the window on a piece of paper. See what happens when you use different convex lenses.

ZOOMING IN AND OUT

You will need: *cardboard tube, thin card (card stock), adhesive tape, scissors, sharp pencil, tracing paper.*

Camera lenses
Some camera lenses consist of several lenses, or elements. As rays of light pass through a lens, they are refracted (bent) at different angles. These rays can distort, resulting in multi-coloured edges on your print. Multiple-element lenses, like the ones seen here, help to prevent the light rays distorting.

1 Cover one end of a cardboard tube with thin card and tape it down. Pierce a small hole in the middle with a sharp pencil.

2 Wrap a large square of card around the other end of the tube. Tape the edge down to form another tube that slides over the first.

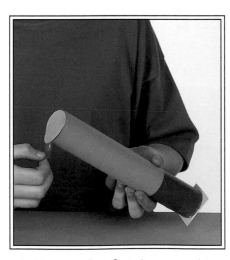

3 Cut a circle of tracing paper big enough to stick over the end of your sliding tube. Tape it firmly in place. This is your focal plane.

Record what you see through your zoom lens. Slide the tubes in and out to make the image bigger (left) or smaller (below).

4 Aim the tube at a window or bright light (with the tracing paper end at your eye). Hold it right up to your eye to get it level with your line of sight, and then move it 10–15cm/4–6in away from your eye. You should now see an image on the tracing paper screen.

Flat and curved mirrors

Some cameras have one or more mirrors instead of a lens. All the rays that hit a mirror are reflected. A flat mirror (*right*) reflects all rays in the same way, so your image looks unchanged (although left and right seem reversed).

A convex mirror reflects and bends light (*left*). It works like a mirror and a lens together to distort the image.

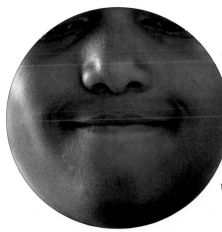

Simple close-ups

Put a small object, such as a coin, on a flat surface. Hold a magnifying glass (the larger, the better) in front of the viewfinder and move the camera until the coin fills about a quarter of the frame. Put the magnifying glass in front of the camera lens and take the photograph. Take a few more shots with the camera a bit nearer and then try moving the camera a bit farther away. A macro lens can be fitted to a camera to take close-ups, and some have a mini-macro lens fitted permanently.

LIGHTING AND FLASH

Lighting is one of the most important parts of photography. The kind of light you take your picture in, how that light hits the subject, and where you take the picture from, all affect the result. Outdoors, most photos are taken with natural light. Artificial light is usually needed indoors, or outdoors when there is not enough natural light. Photographs can be taken in dim natural light without additional artificial light, but only with very long exposures. Lighting can also create dramatic effects. Flash lighting makes a very bright light for a fraction of a second. Most small cameras have a small, built-in flash unit.

Lights and reflectors

Photographic studios have lots of strong lights. They allow the photographer to create many different lighting effects, without worrying about natural light. Some lights make light over a wide area, others make narrow beams. Using umbrellas and sheets of reflecting material can direct the light, too. These can be used to help reduce the contrast on bright sunny days.

With front lighting, light is coming to the subject from the same direction as the camera position or slightly above. It lights the subject evenly, but gives a flat look because there are no strong shadows or highlights.

Back lighting means that the subject is between the light and the camera. It can make your subject look darker. The light does not have to be directly behind. Here, two lights have been set at a 45° angle behind the subject, one on either side.

If a picture is side-lit from the back, then the light is coming across your subject. Side lighting will often give the most interesting or dramatic photographs, because it creates shadows that give more shape and depth to the subject.

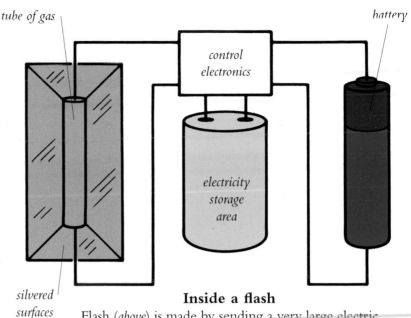

tube of gas

battery

control electronics

electricity storage area

silvered surfaces

Light in a flash

Light from a flash unit only lasts for a fraction of a second. It is carefully timed to flash when the camera's shutter is open. Many cameras have a built-in flash unit. A more powerful flash gun can be added to an SLR camera (*above*). Most cameras have a signal that tells you when you need to use the flash.

Inside a flash

Flash (*above*) is made by sending a very large electric current through a narrow tube of gas. This makes a lightning-like flash. The flash's batteries gradually build up a store of electric charge, which is released very quickly. It is like filling a bowl from a dripping tap and then pouring all the water out at once, or blowing up a balloon and then bursting it.

Bouncing and diffusing

Direct flash from the camera to the subject can cause harsh shadows and red-eye (where the flash creates red reflections in a person's eyes). Bounce flash means aiming the flash at the ceiling, so that the light spreads out. Some photographers diffuse flash with a sheet of material attached to the top of the flash, as on the right.

These people are sitting at different distances from the flash. This means that some of them are overexposed (have too much light), while others are underexposed.

Arrange people so that they are all about the same distance from the camera. This should make sure that everyone is properly exposed.

WORKING WITH LIGHT

Red-eye is caused by light from a flash unit near the camera lens bouncing off the retina (at the back of the eye) and back into the lens. With SLR cameras, the flash can be moved to one side to avoid red-eye. Photo-editing software can remove red-eye from digital images.

Yᵒu can improve many of your photographs by giving thought to the lighting before you shoot. For pictures of people, try some of the simple suggestions here. If you're taking pictures outside, move around your subject to study the effects of light as it falls at different angles. You can also ask people you are photographing to tilt their heads at different angles, so that the sunlight lights up their faces. If there isn't enough light, some cameras have a back light button that lengthens the exposure time for dark subjects. You could also use flash to light up the darker areas. This is known as using fill-in flash.

CREATING LIGHTING EFFECTS

You will need: *a camera, large sheets of white and coloured paper or card (card stock), kitchen foil, desk lamp, torch (flashlight), coloured tissue paper.*

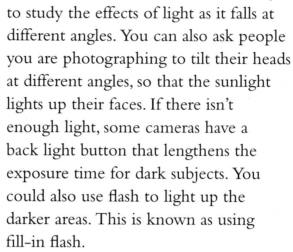

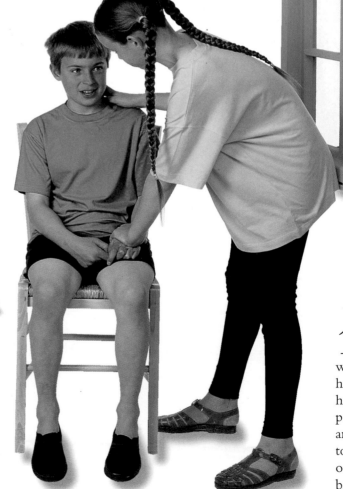

1 Sit your subject near a window and ask him to turn his head into different positions. Move around the room to see the effects of front, side and back lighting.

2 Hold a sheet of white paper or card near your subject to reflect some light from the window back on to his face. The reflected light fills in the shadows caused by the side lighting. Do the same with coloured paper. This will add colour to your subject's face.

3 Try the same with kitchen foil or a piece of shiny card. See how this gives a much brighter reflected light. Crumpling the foil and then smoothing it out again will diffuse the light in interesting and creative ways.

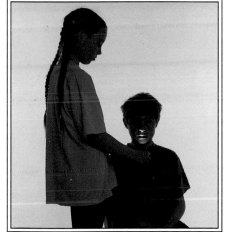

4 For pictures with some really spooky lighting effects, light your subject from below with an ordinary lamp or a torch. Do it in a darkened room with your camera's flash turned off. To try out this kind of effect, you will need to get a friend to help.

5 To take this approach even further, experiment with putting your hand in front of the light. As with the previous step, turn off your camera's flash if you can, and hold the camera very still. If you have a tripod, use that to free your hands.

6 For less harsh lighting, put a sheet of tissue paper in front of the lamp or torch. Try this with coloured tissue paper to see what effects you can achieve. You can also take flash photos with a small piece of tissue paper over the flash unit.

FILTERS AND EFFECTS

A photographic filter changes the light as it enters the camera's lens. There are dozens of different filters, and each one creates its own effect. The most common filter is called a skylight filter. It lets all visible light through the lens but stops invisible ultraviolet light from getting in, as ultraviolet light can make photographs look unnaturally blue. Filters called graduate filters make some parts of the scene darker. They are often used to darken very bright skies. Tinted filters, such as red or yellow, can make black-and-white photographs look very dramatic. The effects that many filters create can be made using photo-editing software on a computer. For example, a sky or clouds can be made darker using digital filters in software.

Normally filters are used only on SLR cameras. Some filters are circular, and screw on to the end of the camera's lens. Others are designed to slot into a filter holder at the front of the lens.

Bright lights
You will not always want strong reflections and bright light in a picture (*right*).

Polarizing filter
Here (*left*), putting a polarizing filter in front of the lens has made the reflections and strong light disappear. These filters cut out certain light rays from a scene, but let others through. They can also have a dramatic effect on skies, making them a much darker blue. If you want to take pictures through a window, a polarizing filter will reduce reflections in the glass.

Creating a sunset

With a sunset filter, you can turn a daytime sky (*left*) into a beautiful sunset (*below*). Half the filter is clear and the other half has a slight orange tint. Position the tint at the top of your shot and the sky appears reddish.

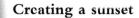

Making your own

You can make filters from transparent tinted confectionery wrappers. Put clean wrappers in front of the camera's viewfinder to see what effect they have. Then attach them to the front of the lens with adhesive tape and rubber bands.

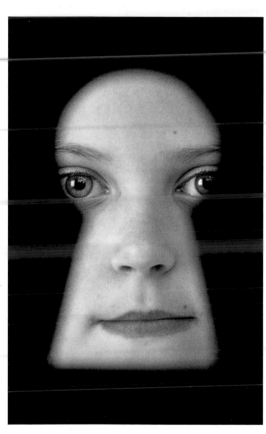

Software mask

You can create lots of filter effects with photo-editing software on a personal computer or tablet. A frame filter creates a shape that your photograph shows through. Frame filters come in simple shapes, such as squares and ovals, and more complex shapes, such as keyholes. Shooting through holes in walls or old trees can give you the same creative effects.

USEFUL TIPS

Once you've got used to taking photographs you will want to take better ones. Here are a few simple tips that should help you to improve your photographic technique and avoid some common mistakes. Good technique is made up of two things: technical skill, which allows you to use your camera to the best of its ability, and an eye for an interesting subject, which will lead you to take photographs that people will enjoy looking at. Always remember that an expensive and complicated camera does not necessarily take the best photographs, and that great shots are perfectly possible with a simple point-and-shoot camera or a smartphone.

Hold a camera steady with both hands. Be careful not to put your fingers over the lens, flash or autofocus sensor. Keep your elbows close to your body and squeeze the shutter release button slowly. Do not stab at it.

Check the background

When you are taking portraits, or photographs of groups of people, always look at the background as well as at your subject. If necessary, recompose your picture to avoid the sort of accident that has happened in this shot. Many cameras have a portrait setting that gives a shallow depth of field. This automatically makes the background go out of focus.

Fill the frame

Do not be afraid to get close to your subject. For example, if you are taking a portrait, make sure the person's head and shoulders fill the frame (*right*). But be careful not to get too close, because the camera may not be able to focus (*far right*). If you get too close with an autofocus camera, it will not let you take a picture.

Natural frames
Try adding some interest to photos by shooting through archways or doors to frame the subject. With photos of groups or scenery, you can include overhanging branches in the foreground.

The rule of thirds
Try using the rule of thirds: place the subject a third of the way across or up or down the frame. This makes the shot more interesting. With autofocus cameras, you often have to use your focus lock to point at the subject first and then recompose the picture before shooting. Try this with landscapes, for example, having a mountain range in the top third of the frame.

A different viewpoint
Photographs taken from a standing position have the same viewpoint as your eyes usually do. Changing the camera's viewpoint can give more interesting results. Try kneeling, or even lying down.

Bad weather photographs
You do not always need to wait for good weather before taking photos. In fact, overhead sunshine tends to give flat, dull pictures. Stormy clouds can be much more interesting than cloudless skies. Remember to protect your camera in extreme weather conditions to make sure it stays dry.

SPECIAL PHOTOGRAPHY

Most cameras and lenses are designed for general photography, such as taking pictures of landscapes or people. However, there are some types of camera designed to take photographs in special conditions, or in unusual formats. For example, some cameras and smartphones are completely waterproof, for taking pictures underwater, many cameras can take very wide photographs, called panoramas, and 3-D cameras can take three-dimensional photographs, which have to be viewed through 3-D glasses for full effect. Special cameras and lenses are also used in scientific and environmental work.

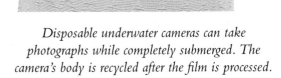

Disposable underwater cameras can take photographs while completely submerged. The camera's body is recycled after the film is processed.

Underwater SLRs

Divers take photographs underwater with special SLR cameras that are waterproof even when they are many metres down. They can also withstand the high pressure of being in deep water. Special housings are available for many cameras to enable land cameras to be used underwater or in adverse conditions, such as during a cave diving or pot-holing expedition.

It's a really good idea to have an underwater camera for a pool party or a beach holiday.

Super-wide photographs

A panorama is a very wide picture. Photographers use panoramas to take dramatic shots of the landscape, or photographs of large groups of people. Many digital cameras and smartphones will automatically take panoramas for you, or you can take several photographs and join them side by side.

Laser photographs

A hologram is a three-dimensional (3-D) picture that looks 3-D no matter what angle you look at it from. The picture changes as you move your head from side to side. However, holograms are not taken with a camera. Another kind of equipment is used to record how laser light bounces off the subject from different directions.

FACT BOX

• Some smartphones are waterproof and have very good cameras, so they can take excellent underwater photographs.

• Many digital cameras can analyse the scene your camera is pointing at and automatically detect that you want to take a panoramic shot.

• DSLR cameras can be put on a motorized tripod, which turns the camera slowly to take a series of panoramic photographs.

3-D cameras

You can get cameras that take 3-D, or stereo, photographs. The images can be printed out to make a stereo pair, or viewed on a 3-D television using special glasses. A 3-D camera has two lenses and two sensors, positioned slightly apart. There are also 3-D lens caps that can be fitted to regular SLR and DSLR cameras.

AMAZING EFFECTS

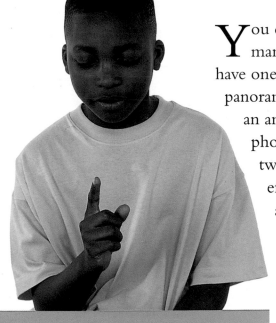

You can get 3-D cameras that take 3-D (stereo) photographs, and many cameras can take panoramic photographs. But if you don't have one of these cameras, you can still create stereo photographs and panoramic photographs with a digital camera and a printer. To get an amazing stereo photograph, all you have to do is take two photographs of the same scene from different angles. Place the two printed photos side by side to see the three-dimensional effect for yourself. The effect works because, like many animals, humans have binocular vision. This means that the two different views from our two eyes overlap. You can also make a wide panorama by taking a series of photographs, printing them out and joining them together.

Place your stereo pair of photographs side by side to view them.

The diagram on the right shows how the stereo effect is created – because our two eyes see slightly different views.

left eye sees this view

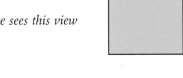

right eye sees this view

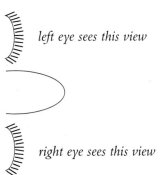

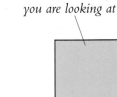

the actual 3-D box you are looking at

MAKE YOUR MODEL COME ALIVE

1 Choose a simple object such as this model of a dinosaur. Holding the camera very steady, take a picture. Try to include a little space around your subject.

2 Step about 20cm/8in to your left, and take another photo. Try taking more pairs of photographs, using different distances between the two photographs.

You will need:
camera, model.

3 Put your pictures down side by side on a flat surface. Stand over them and place your index finger between the two. With your eyes directly above the photos, look down at the finger and slowly raise it towards your nose, keeping it in focus. The two images you see below should merge into one 3-D image.

Make a panorama

Choose a good general landscape scene, with no close-up objects in it. Now take a series of photographs that overlap slightly. Set a zoom lens at medium length for this. Start by looking towards your left and move your head slightly round to the right for each of the following shots. When your photos are printed, lay them out in the right order to recreate all of your scene. When you are happy with the arrangement, tape them together carefully. You could also place digital photographs next to each other on your computer screen for viewing.

This completed panorama (above) works well because it is a simple, open scene. If it had been filled with small objects, then the effect might not have been so good. If you want people in your scene, try to keep them away from areas that will overlap in the finished panorama. On the other hand, you could ask a friend to move into different parts of the scene for each different shot and produce a picture with multiple images of him or her.

MOVING PICTURES

Most digital cameras and smartphones can record videos as well as take photographs. A video is made up of many individual images, called frames. The camera records around 25 frames every second, and stores them on a memory card. When the frames are displayed quickly on a screen, one after the other, the movement in the original scene appears to be recreated. Before digital cameras became popular, people used video cameras, which recorded video images on magnetic tape. Some are still in use. Before that, moving pictures were captured on strips of film, using a cine camera. Today, cine cameras are used mainly for professional movie-making.

Moving images rely on the fact that we have persistence of vision. This means our eyes remember a picture for a split second. To see how this works, look at a scene and close your eyes quickly.

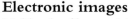

Recording motion

The early movie cameras grew out of experiments to record and study animal motion rather than for entertainment. This sequence (*left*) was taken by British photographer Eadweard Muybridge (1830–1904). He had first come up with the idea of moving pictures in 1877 after taking a series of photographs of a horse running, using 24 different cameras. Muybridge produced hundreds of images recording the complex movements of animals and humans which were too quick for the unaided human eye to follow.

Film and cine cameras

Cine film is just like the rolls of film you put in a stills camera, but a lot longer! Inside a cine camera the film is wound on, ready to take the next frame, while the shutter is closed. The shutter speed is always the same and the exposure is controlled just by the aperture.

Electronic images

Unlike the film used in cine cameras, the earliest video cameras (or camcorders) used tape with a magnetic coating. Such cameras do not record the amount of light in a scene, as a film camera would. Instead, pictures are recorded by an electronic signal which distorts the tape. A video player can read this signal and reproduce the image.

Digital video cameras

There are digital video cameras that are dedicated to recording video rather than single photographs. These range from large cameras with long zoom lenses used by television professionals and film-makers, to tiny, cheap video cameras that you can carry around in your pocket. Most cameras record high-definition video on to memory chips. They record high-quality sound as well as pictures. Most cameras on smartphones also have a video-making option.

Snowboarders and mountain bikers enjoy making videos of their downhill runs and stunts with helmet-mounted video cameras. City cyclists also now sometimes wear cameras like these so that they can make a record of any bad driving that might endanger them.

Editing and sharing videos

Digital videos can easily be downloaded from cameras to computers and edited to make finished videos. As with photos, videos can be shown on computer screens, and can be uploaded to video-sharing websites on the internet, where anyone can watch them.

FACT BOX

• The fastest movie cameras are used by scientists. They can take up to 4.4 trillion frames every second. If you used a camera like this to record a bullet fired from a gun, the bullet would take over 7,000 frames to travel just one millimetre.

• An IMAX cinema screen is as tall as seven elephants on top of each other. IMAX film is four times larger than 35mm film.

• The earliest regular television broadcasts, started by the BBC in 1936, had 405 horizontal lines of resolution. By comparison, a modern ultra-high-definition TV screen can display 2160 lines.

High-speed video

This is a frame from a high-speed video. Some video cameras can record hundreds, or even thousands, of frames every second. When they are played back at normal speed, the action is slowed right down.

ANIMATION

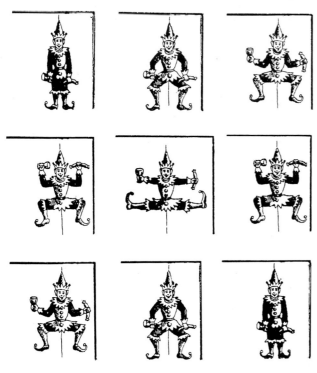

Animation is making inanimate objects, or objects that cannot move by themselves, appear to move. Frames of a video film are photographed one at a time with a special video camera or cine camera that can take one frame at a time. Between each frame, the objects are moved slightly. Sometimes this is combined with camera movement or zoom effects. When the finished video is viewed, the objects seem to move. Some animated objects are models, which are photographed to make animated movies. Others are drawings, which are photographed to make cartoons. Modern cartoon animation is often done by computer, so the photography stage is not needed. Quite often only the main drawings are made by an artist and a computer plans the movements and frames using animation software.

Photo flick-book

The simplest way of making moving pictures is to put all the frames into a book and flick through the pages. In the early 1800s, flick books of photographs (called filoscopes) were used to entertain children as movies had not yet been invented. You can see some of the pages from an old filoscope above.

Turning marvel

A thaumotrope is a double-sided disc, often made of cardboard, which has partial pictures on either side. When you spin the disc, the pictures appear to merge. So, if you had a bird on one side and a cage on the other, when the disc was spun you would see the bird in the cage. The name 'thaumotrope' comes from the Greek words for marvel and turning.

This picture shows a scene from one of the popular Wallace and Gromit films, made by Aardman Animations Ltd. Model animation is a highly skilful and time-consuming job. The models must be moved very, very slightly between each frame. There are around 25 frames for every second of film.

FACT BOX

• A video camera used for shooting cels is fixed so that it looks down on a flat baseboard. The cels for one frame are placed on the board and a photo is taken. Then the cels for the next frame are shot, and so on.

• Model animation is done with a camera, held firm on a rostrum, or platform, so that it does not shift between frames. However, it can be tilted, panned (moved to follow a moving object) and zoomed to create different effects.

• A 20-minute animated video uses between 15,000 and 30,000 frames.

This picture appears in the top right-hand corner of every other page in this part of the book. Flick all the pages of this section quickly and watch the pictures. What can you see happening?

Enjoying animation

Producing animated children's films is big business. Many cartoons are made with the aid of computers. Some computer packages do all the time-consuming drawing and painting. They can also produce complex, three-dimensional characters, or add cartoon elements to film of real actors. In special effects scenes, real actors may be replaced by computer-generated images of themselves.

Background cels

Cartoon cels

Until the 1980s, cartoon films were made by photographing a series of drawings. The drawings were done on transparent plastic sheets called cels. Moving characters were drawn on one cel and the still background on another, to save drawing the background again and again for each frame. Once the cels were completed, they were photographed with a cine camera. When these were shown in rapid succession, a moving film appeared.

Character cels (notice how each one is different either in expression or the clothing)

EASY ANIMATION

During the 1800s, there was a craze for optical toys, such as flick-books. Many of them created an illusion of movement by displaying a sequence of pictures in quick succession. At first, the pictures were hand-drawn. Later, photos taken by early movie cameras were used as well. Here, you can find out how to make a toy called a phenakistoscope, and how to use it to turn a series of pictures into animation. Our toy is slightly different from the Victorian one shown on the right, as it has slots cut around the edges of the circle, rather than in the middle.

A phenakistoscope (above) was an early device used to view moving pictures in a mirror. It held a set of images that were all slightly different. When you spun the disc, you saw an action sequence through the slots.

A series of simple drawings work best for this kind of animation. This strip of images is for a zoetrope.

MAKE YOUR OWN PHENAKISTOSCOPE

You will need: *thick, dark card (card stock), pencil, ruler, scissors, white paper, dark felt-tip marker, tape, camera, models.*

1 On the card, draw a circle, 26cm/10in across. Divide it into eight equal segments. At the end of each segment line, draw slots 4cm/2in long and 5mm/¼in wide.

2 Now cut out your disc, and the evenly spaced slots around the outside of it. Make sure that the slots are no wider than 5mm/¼in. These will be your viewing holes.

3 On pieces of white paper, draw a series of eight pictures. These should form a sequence of movements. Make sure that your drawings are fairly simple and clear, and that they are drawn with clean, strong lines.

4 Attach the little drawings to the disc by taping them just under the slots. You may need to cut them to fit, but make sure the picture is positioned below the slot. Push a pencil through the middle of the card disc to make a handle.

5 Stand in front of a mirror. Hold the disc vertically, with the pictures toward the mirror. Spin the disc and look through the slots. You should see an animated loop of action in the mirror.

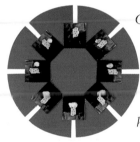

Once you have mastered the technique of making a photo phenakistoscope, you can get more adventurous with your subjects and story lines. Try adding more models or props, for example putting hats on the models.

PHOTO PHENAKISTOSCOPE

1 Now try a model animation. Take eight photographs of a model from the same position (use a tripod if you can). Move the model(s) slightly each time. The models should take up the middle third of the photograph frame.

2 Cut your photos to size and stick them to the phenakistoscope, one photo underneath each slot. Your phenakistoscope will work better if the photos have a dark frame, or you can just cover the edges roughly with a black felt-tip marker pen.

A zoetrope
This zoetrope from the 1860s was used to display long strips of drawings showing simple action sequences. They were placed inside a cylinder that could be rotated by hand. The moving pictures were then viewed through the vertical slots cut in the cylinder.

CAMERAS IN SCIENCE

Some advanced microscopes (above) can take very detailed close-up photos. You can also do the same thing with a normal microscope, by fitting a DSLR camera to it. You remove the DSLR's lens and the microscope acts as a close-up lens for the camera.

Most of us use our cameras for recording outings and special occasions, or for taking pictures of our friends. However, photography is also extremely important in science and technology. For example, it is used for recording images that have been made by scientific instruments, so that they can be studied later. It can also be used to record experiments that happen too fast or at too small a scale for the human eye to see, as well as for analysing experimental results. Most scientific instruments use digital cameras rather than film, so that their images can be transferred easily to computers for analysis.

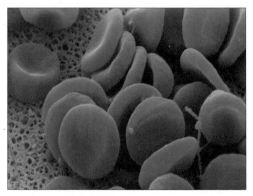

Microscope photographs
A photograph taken using a microscope is called a photomicrograph. This one is a close-up of the red blood cells in our blood.

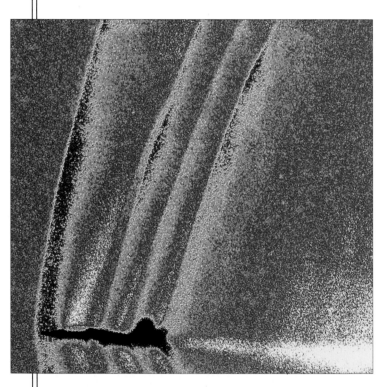

Recording speed on camera
This type of photograph is known as a schlieren photograph. It shows the shock waves around a T-38 aircraft flying at great speed – 1.1 times the speed of sound, or Mach 1.1. The waves appear as red and green diagonal lines in the photograph. It enables scientists to see that the main shock waves come from the nose and tail of the plane. Smaller shock waves come from the engine inlets and wings. The yellow stream behind the aircraft is caused by the exhaust of the jet engine.

Photographing heat
All objects give off heat rays called infrared rays. Hotter objects give off stronger rays. A special type of film called infrared film is sensitive to heat rays rather than light rays. Hot and cold objects show up in different colours or shades.

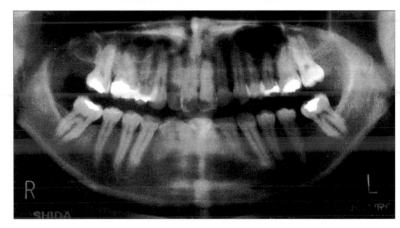

When you are taking photos of the sky with a telescope using long exposures, the telescope often has to move slowly across the sky. This is to prevent the stars from becoming streaks on your prints. This happens because the Earth and stars are slowly moving. It is like taking a picture of a traffic light from a moving car. The lights would appear streaked.

Seeing stars

Just as a camera can be added to a microscope to take close-up pictures, one can also be added to a telescope. The telescope acts like a very powerful telephoto lens for the camera. (A telephoto lens makes distant objects seem much closer.) Light from the stars is very weak, and so long exposures are needed.

Where more X-rays reach the film, through soft parts of the body, the film turns a darker tone when it is developed. Bones and teeth show up white.

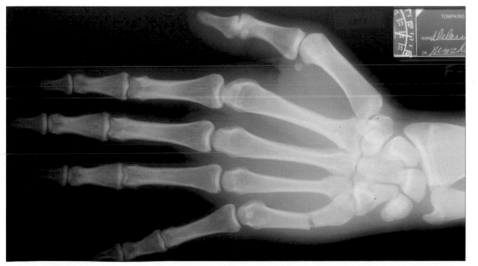

Taking X-ray pictures

X-rays are used to photograph inside bodies. Unlike light rays, X-rays can pass though the soft parts of your body – skin and muscle. X-ray machines use either digital sensors or X-ray film. X-rays help dentists or doctors to find out all kinds of things about the body. The picture on the left shows the hand of a boxer with a fractured finger caused through punching. Other kinds of X-ray technology are used to scan for faults in the structure of buildings or aircraft, enabling repairs to take place before a part fails or causes an accident.

GLOSSARY

aperture
In most cameras the aperture is a hole behind the lens which can be adjusted to let more or less light on to the sensor or film.

APS (Advanced Photographic System) camera
Camera that allows you to change the format for individual shots.

autofocus
A feature on a camera which automatically adjusts the lens position to make sure a scene is in focus.

CCD
Short for charge-coupled device, which is a type of image sensor.

camera obscura
A darkened box or room in which images of outside objects are projected.

cloud
In cloud computing, files and programs are stored on the internet rather than on individual computers.

CMOS
Short for complementary metal-oxide semiconductor, which is used to make image sensors.

converging (or convex) lens
A lens that curves outwards, as on a magnifying glass. This causes rays of light from an object to bend inwards and makes things seem larger.

conversion filter
A filter that can be attached to a camera to produce a natural lighting effect when you are taking pictures indoors.

depth of field
The distance between the nearest and farthest parts of the scene that are in focus at one time.

diffraction
The scattering of light rays.

diffuser
A filter, similar to a sheet of tissue paper, than can be attached to a camera to soften light from a flash.

digital camera
A camera that takes electronic images which are downloaded on to a computer to be viewed.

diverging lens
A lens that causes causes rays of light from an object to spread outwards.

download
To move an image (or other computer file) from a camera, smartphone or the internet to a computer.

DSLR
A digital SLR camera (*see SLR*).

endoscope
A long, slender camera attachment that goes inside the body to take pictures of internal organs and relays the images to a computer screen.

exposures
Photographs on a film. An exposure generally refers to a single shutter cycle.

exposure time
The time it takes for the camera to take a picture. This is the time a shutter is open letting light from the scene hit the lens.

fill-in flash
Using the flash to light up certain areas of your picture, but leaving natural light in the background.

filter
Transparent material fitted to a lens that alters the colour of the light or the way the light rays pass through it.

fish-eye lens
A very wide-angle lens that collects light from 180 degrees. The middle of the scene looks much bigger.

flash
A bulb attached to the camera that provides a quick burst of light so that a picture can be taken in darkness.

focal length
The distance between the middle of a lens and the focal point – the point where light rays enter.

focal plane
The area at the back of a camera where the exposed film is held flat. It is the point at which the light rays meet.

focus
A camera is in focus when the light rays from an object meet on the focal plane to form a sharp image of the scene.

format
The size and shape of a print and the way it can be viewed (as a print, a slide or on a computer, for example).

frame
The area seen through the viewfinder.

frame filter
Black material with a hole cut in the middle, such as a keyhole or circle, that fits over the lens. The scene will come out inside that shape on the print, the covered area will be black.

image sensor
An electronic chip inside a digital camera that is sensitive to light and records the image made by the lens.

infra-red light
Rays of light that are invisible because they have a wavelength that is longer than the red end of the part of the light spectrum we can see.

ISO rating
A rating system for film which tells you the speed. For example, an ISO 200 film is twice as fast as an ISO 100 film. ISO stands for International Standards Organization.

laser light
A narrow and powerful beam of light produced by a laser machine, used in making holograms, video discs and cutting equipment, among other things.

latent image
Invisible image produced by light hitting the silver crystals in film.

leaf shutter
A shutter that is made up of a number of overlapping plates which retract to open.

lens
A transparent material that is curved on one or both sides. It bends rays of light from an object and directs them on to the sensor or film.

light spectrum
The colours that light can be split into. The light spectrum is part of the electromagnetic spectrum which includes light rays, sound rays, microwaves, radio waves, X-rays and Gamma rays.

macro lens
A close-up lens that has very short focal length, used to take pictures of objects very close to the camera.

memory card
A small plastic card that contains memory chips that can be plugged into a camera for storing image files.

monochrome
Black-and-white film or photographic paper, it shows colours as shades of black/grey.

negative
The photographic image on the developed film from which prints will be made. The colours or tones are reversed, so dark areas look light and light areas look dark.

over-exposure
Where the subject of a photograph appears dark. It is caused by not enough light rays from the subject hitting the sensor or film.

panoramic picture
A photograph showing an extra wide view of a scene such as a landscape.

pixels
Tiny dots that make up a digital image.

polarizing filter
A filter put in front of a lens to cut out reflections from water, glass or metal.

Polaroid camera
A type of camera that can take and develop individual prints immediately as it has developing chemicals inside.

positive
A print or slide showing a photographic image with colours or tones which are the same as in the original scene.

primary colours
Three colours – red, blue and green or cyan, magenta and yellow. When mixed together, they make any other colour.

prism
Specially shaped glass used to split white light into the spectrum, or reflect light rays away from their normal path.

reflectors
A sheet of reflecting material or umbrella used to light a subject.

refraction
The bending of light rays.

reversal film or slide film
A film that, when developed, gives a positive image, known as a transparency.

rostrum
A platform used to hold a film or video camera still during shooting.

shutter
Camera mechanism, like a little door, which opens and shuts to control the amount of time during which light falls on to the lens.

SLR (Single Lens Reflex)
A design of camera that allows you to see exactly what the lens sees. A digital version is called a DSLR.

stills photography
Photography showing a single image (as opposed to recording moving images).

telephoto lens
A lens which takes a close-up picture of a distant scene.

tripod
A camera stand with three legs.

tungsten film
Film designed to be used inside. It reproduces light from a lamp or indoor light as if it was white so the pictures do not look yellowy.

ultra-violet light
Rays of light that are invisible to our eyes because they have a wavelength that is shorter than the blue end of the part of the light spectrum we can see.

under-exposure
A photograph that looks washed out as too much light from the subject has hit the sensor or film.

upload
To move an image file (or other computer file) from a computer, tablet, camera or smartphone to a server on the internet.

viewfinder
The window you look through to see what will be in your photograph.

wide-angle lens
Lens with an angle of view that is wider than normal for the human eye.

wi-fi
A system that allows cameras, smartphones, tablets and computers to join a network using wireless radio waves rather than cables.

X-ray photographs
Pictures taken of the inside of our bodies, used to show broken bones.

zoom lens
A lens with a variable focal length, so that you can alter it to get in close to a distant subject or use as a normal lens.

INDEX

A
animation 56-9
aperture 24-5, 28-9
  and exposure 26
  shutter speed and 27
APS (Advanced
  Photographic System)
  system 27, 51
autofocus cameras 12, 13,
  48, 49

B
back lighting 27, 42, 44
black-and-white film 16
  filters 46
  printing 30
  processing 17

C
camera obscura 8, 9
cartoons 56, 57
cassettes, film 6
chemicals, films 16
cine cameras 54-5, 56, 57
close-up shots 7, 38-9, 41
colour filters 46, 47
colour negative film 31
colour reversal film 16, 17
compact cameras 6, 7, 22,
  37, 38, 40
computers 56, 57
crystals, film 16-17

D
depth of field 24, 25, 28, 48
developer 20, 30
developing film 16, 17, 30

disposable cameras 6, 15,
  46, 51
download 30, 55, 62
D3LR (digital single lens
  reflex camera) 4, 11, 12,
  38, 39, 51, 60

E
early cameras 4
electronic cameras 56
exposure 16, 26-7

F
f-numbers 24, 25
fill-in flash 44-5
film 5, 16-17
  developing 16, 30
  exposing 16
  loading 6, 16, 48
  movie cameras 54, 55
  processing 17
  single-use cameras 15
  types of 16
filters 19, 46-7
fish-eye lenses 36
fixer 17, 30
flash 5, 42, 43, 44
focal length 24, 25, 36-7,
  38-9, 40-1
focal plane 12, 36
focal-plane shutters 22,
  28, 29
focus 12-13, 24-5, 48
focus lock 13, 49
Fox Talbot, William 31
frame filters 47
front lighting 42

H
high-speed photos 55
holograms 51

I
image sensors 20
infra-red film 60

L
laser photographs 51
leaf shutters 22, 28
lenses 6, 8-9
  aperture 24-5
  filters 46-7
  fish-eye 36

focal length 36-7, 38-9
focusing 12-13
light refraction 10
macro 38, 41
shutters 22
telephoto 5, 36, 37, 38, 61
wide-angle lenses 37
zoom lenses 37, 38, 40
light
  aperture 24-5
  exposure 26-7
  film 16
  filters 46-7
  flash 42, 43, 44
  focus 12
  light rays 8-9
  lighting 42-3
  photograms 18-19
  reflection 10-11, 41, 45
  refraction 10, 40
  shutters 22

M
macro lenses 38, 41
magnifying glasses 10, 12,
  28, 34, 35, 41
memory cards 21
metering systems 26
mini-labs, processing 5, 31
mirrors 10-11, 41
monochrome paper 21
monopods 36
motors, electric 6, 13
movie cameras 54-5, 56, 57
Muybridge, Eadweard 54

N
negatives 5, 17, 30

P
panning 23
panoramic photos 37,
  51, 53
phenakistoscopes 58-9
photograms 20-1
photomicrographs 60
pin-hole cameras 8-9, 14-
  15, 25, 34
pixels 20, 21
polarizing filters 46
Polaroid cameras 7
portraits 43, 44-5, 48, 51
prints 5, 16, 30-3

processing film 17
projectors 30, 34, 35, 54

R
red-eye 43, 44
reflection, light 10-11,
  41, 45
refraction, light 10, 40

S
selfies 33
shutters 4, 6, 22-3, 28-9
  cine cameras 55
  speed 22, 23, 26, 27, 36
side lighting 42
skylight filters 46
slides
  film 16, 17
  projectors 30, 34, 35
SLR (single lens reflex
  camera) 7, 48
social media 32, 33
special-effect filters 46
stereo photos 50, 51, 52-3
super-zoom lenses 38

T
telephoto lenses 5, 36, 37,
  39, 61
3-D cameras 50, 51, 52-3
35mm cameras 7, 37
35mm film 54
tripods 5, 23, 36

U
ultra-violet light 46
under-exposure 26, 27, 43
underwater cameras 50
upload 30, 31, 33, 55, 63

V
video cameras 54, 56
viewers 8-9, 34

W
water mirrors 11
wide-angle lenses 37

X
X-ray film 61

Z
zoom lenses 37, 38, 40